picnics

picnics

Easy Recipes for the Best Alfresco Foods

ROBIN VITETTA-MILLER

Clarkson Potter/Publishers
New York

For Darrin, Kyle, and Luke

Published by Clarkson Potter/Publishers, New York, New York.
Member of the Crown Publishing Group, a division of Random House, Inc.
www.crownpublishing.com

CLARKSON N. POTTER is a trademark and POTTER and colophon are registered trademarks of Random House, Inc.

Printed in Singapore

Design by Maggie Hinders

Library of Congress Cataloging-in-Publication Data
Vitetta-Miller, Robin, 1964–
    Picnics : easy recipes for the best alfresco foods / Robin Vitetta-Miller.
        p.   cm.
1. Picnicking. I. Title.
TX823 .V58   2004
641.5'78—dc21   2003004587

ISBN 1-4000-4696-3

10 9 8 7 6 5 4 3 2 1

First Edition

contents

introduction

Picnic: 1. *an excursion or outing with food, usually eaten in the open;* 2. *a pleasant or amusingly carefree experience.*

WELL, THAT PRETTY MUCH SUMS IT UP: an amusing journey bursting with savory treats for feasting. But we're not talking about the picnic; we're referring to the cookbook. Immerse yourself in these pages and you'll find sensational salads, sandwiches, wraps, dips, breads, cookies, bars, cakes, and more. Each dish was created with alfresco dining in mind, and every recipe in Picnics is straightforward and simple to prepare. The fact is that outdoor feasts are meant to be fun, so leave those visions of complicated meals at the kitchen door.

Make sure to read the headnote at the beginning of each recipe. These suggestions for storage, wrapping, and packing aren't merely for maintaining the flavor and texture of your dish: The right food handling will prevent spoilage and contamination. (After all that work, we'd hate to ruin the party!)

You'll find something for any occasion— from autumn in the park to a summer beach party. Pick the occasion, try the sample menus, and get packing. Bad weather? Not to worry: Throw a blanket on the floor and dine under the glorious light of your family room.

the best alfresco foods

Some foods simply stand the test of time and travel better than others. For example, handheld wrapped sandwiches make better picnic fare than, say, gazpacho. The best choices? Finger foods, premixed salads, sandwiches and wraps, dips, breads, and cookies and bars. When planning a picnic, consider:

✳ HOW YOU'LL BE TRANSPORTING THE FOOD. Foods cannot stay as cold in a basket as they can in a cooler. Stick to foods whose risk of bacterial contamination is low (pasta salad, fruit salad, vegetarian wrap sandwiches, dips).

✳ WHETHER THE FOOD WILL BE EASY TO TRANSPORT. Sandwiches wrap up tightly in plastic wrap, dips can be spooned into sealable plastic containers, fruit can be tossed into resealable plastic bags, and breads can be carried alongside the cooler.

✳ HOW LONG THE FOOD WILL SIT BEFORE YOU EAT. Make sure you pack so that the food can stay cold the entire time. If your ice melts, the food has just one hour before you need to toss it. If you still have ice, the food's still safe to eat.

* WHETHER THE FOOD CAN BE SERVED AT ROOM TEMPERATURE OR WARMER. Perfect example: Chicken salad should be served cold; pasta salad (without meat) can be served warm.
* HOW FAR IN ADVANCE YOU WANT TO PREPARE THE FOOD. Don't prepare food more than one day before the picnic, unless you plan to freeze it. Cooking food in advance gives bacteria a greater opportunity to grow.

wrapping and packing

The most important aspect of packing the cooler actually occurs before you begin piling in the food: Cooked food must be cooled completely before packing. To speed up the cooling process, spread food out in several containers so that it reaches no more than 2 inches up the sides of the container (you can always transfer cooled foods to smaller containers later).

You'll find that sealable plastic containers are a picnicker's best friend. Most dishes work exceptionally well in these containers, and they're not too deep (so you can chill the food in them right from the beginning). Resealable plastic bags are great for cookies, bars, toasts, nuts, and other dry foods. Bags are also great for cut-up fruit pieces.

PACKING THE COOLER

Pack cold foods in a sturdy, insulated container with plenty of ice or frozen gel packs. To make your own ice packs, freeze water in empty milk cartons or plastic containers. If the food is in sealable plastic containers, wrap the containers in plastic wrap or aluminum foil before adding them to the cooler. When you are ready to pack, move the chilled food immediately from the refrigerator and completely immerse the containers in the ice. When using frozen gel packs or containers of homemade ice, place the food between the packs—never just set food on top of the ice or ice packs.

If you're bringing raw meat, fish, or poultry, pack it in the bottom of the cooler to prevent the meat juices from dripping onto other foods.

KEEP IT FRESH, KEEP IT BEST

Ants are a given at any picnic—they're at least visible. But food poisoning isn't. Don't worry; there are several steps you can take to ensure a safe, bacteria-free feast.

* Food lasts just two hours between the temperatures of 40°F. and 140°F. Chances are your picnic will fall in this range. Under 40°F. is refrigeration and over 140°F. is cooking, and those two options are typically impossible in a field or on a beach. Leftovers should be returned to the cooler immediately after they're served. Food on tables should be covered to prevent contamination by insects.
* Thanks to the addition of preservatives, many condiments (including mayonnaise) actually preserve food and prevent bacterial

contamination. Who knew? Mayo gets a bad rap because back when folks made the creamy spread from scratch, with raw eggs, it was the food-poisoning culprit more times than not. The truth is that mayonnaise alone is too acidic for bacteria to grow in. But when mayo is mixed with other foods, especially high-protein foods such as chicken and tuna, bacteria can run rampant if the temperature is right (40°–140°F.).

* If you're planning to have takeout (fried chicken, barbecued beef, egg salad), eat the food within one to two hours of picking it up, or buy the food ahead of time and thoroughly chill everything in the refrigerator before packing.

* Most people don't realize that melon (watermelon, cantaloupe, honeydew) is the cause of many foodborne illnesses. Unlike most fruits, melon isn't acidic, so it easily supports the growth of harmful bacteria. And those bacteria love to hang out on the melon's rind—meaning that when you cut through to the flesh, the bacteria follow the knife. So wash melon thoroughly before slicing it, and then refrigerate the cut pieces, either in sealable plastic containers or resealable plastic bags, until you're ready to pack them into a cold cooler.

* When you get home, if there's still ice in the cooler, the food is still safe. If all the ice has melted, toss the food.

KEEP IT CLEAN
Wash your hands before handling all food, and use clean utensils and dishware. Dirty hands and utensils can quickly contaminate food with harmful bacteria and viruses. If you think you may have trouble finding a sink, pack anti-bacterial wipes.

KEEP IT COLD
The trunk of your car can reach temperatures of 150°F. (not great for ice), so transport the cooler in the backseat of your air-conditioned car. When you get to the picnic site, place the cooler in the shade and cover it with a blanket. Replenish the cooler with ice as often as necessary. Pack beverages in a separate cooler because the cooler with drinks is opened constantly. And try to keep all coolers packed—full coolers stay colder than half-empty ones.

basket blunders
The fruit salad is too cold, the chicken salad is too warm, the sandwiches are soggy, and the cookies are rock hard. Ever been there? These mistakes are common, but they're also preventable. Here's how to avoid common picnic pitfalls:

* Keep foods cold by packing the cooler straight from the refrigerator.

* To keep all foods equally cold, arrange food and ice in layers—don't rest the food on top of the ice or nestle it underneath.

* Don't underpack the cooler. A fully packed cooler stays colder than a half-empty one. Buy a smaller cooler if you need to.
* To prevent leaking, pack wet items (fruit salads and dips) in sealed plastic containers. "Burp" the container by lifting one corner to allow air to escape before sealing it completely.
* Items that you want to serve at room temperature (not ice-cold) should be packed last and removed first.
* To keep sandwiches from becoming soggy, wrap them in plastic, and then place them in resealable plastic bags. To prevent soggy bread, separate bread and "wet ingredients" (such as tomato slices) with dry lettuce leaves.
* To keep cookies moist, place them in a sealable plastic container and add a few fresh apple slices or a piece of bread (the cookies will pull moisture from the apple and/or bread and stay moist).
* To keep cakes and quick breads moist, wait until the picnic to slice them.

EXTRAS WORTH REMEMBERING
Some items just scream "Leave me behind." Don't. Grab these extras on the way out the door and you'll be glad you did:

* A bottler opener (for both corks and bottle tops)
* Paper towels
* Bug spray
* Trash bags
* Antibacterial wipes
* Water

ONE

finger foods and starters

- Smoky Chicken Fingers with Creamy Honey-Mustard Dip

- Thai Noodles with Vegetables and Peanuts

- Red Potato Salad with Bacon and Fresh Herbs

- Smoked Salmon with Caper Sour Cream and Black Bread

- Coriander Peanut Sauce with Crudités

- Mini Crab Cakes with Wasabi Mayonnaise

- Minty Cucumber Salad

- Mango Salad with Tomatoes and Red Onion

Smoky Chicken Fingers
with Creamy Honey-Mustard Dip

SERVES 4

FOR THE CHICKEN
Cooking spray

¹/₃ cup all-purpose flour

¹/₂ teaspoon salt

**¹/₄ teaspoon freshly ground
black pepper**

¹/₂ cup whole milk

1 teaspoon liquid smoke

1 cup seasoned dry bread crumbs

**1 pound skinless chicken tenders
(rib meat) or skinless,
boneless chicken breast,
cut into 1-inch-wide strips**

FOR THE DIP
1 cup sour cream

2 tablespoons Dijon mustard

2 tablespoons honey

PACKING: Wrap the chicken fingers in plastic wrap and store them in a sealable plastic container or a resealable plastic bag. Store the dip in a sealable plastic container. Keep both refrigerated until you're ready to pack them into a cold cooler.

Preheat the oven to 400°F.

Coat a large baking sheet with cooking spray.

In a shallow bowl, combine the flour, salt, and pepper; mix with a fork to combine. In another shallow bowl, combine the milk and liquid smoke. Place the bread crumbs in a third shallow bowl. Dip the chicken strips into the flour mixture and turn to coat both sides; shake off the excess. Transfer the chicken to the milk mixture and turn to coat both sides, then coat both sides with the bread crumbs. Place the breaded chicken on the prepared baking sheet and spray the chicken strips with cooking spray. Bake for 25 minutes, until the chicken is cooked through.

Meanwhile, in a medium bowl, whisk together the sour cream, mustard, and honey. Serve the chicken with the dip on the side.

Thai Noodles with Vegetables and Peanuts

SERVES 4

PACKING: Store the noodles in a sealable plastic container in the refrigerator until you're ready to pack them into a cold cooler. Top with the peanuts just before serving.

Cook the noodles according to package directions. Drain, transfer to a large bowl, and add the red and green bell peppers, carrots, and scallions. Toss to combine.

In a medium bowl, whisk together the chicken broth, soy sauce, peanut butter, sesame oil, hot sauce, and ginger. Add to the noodles and toss to combine. Sprinkle the peanuts over the top just before serving.

1 pound uncooked somen noodles

1 red bell pepper, seeded and diced

1 green bell pepper, seeded and diced

10 baby carrots, cut into matchsticks

2 tablespoons chopped scallions (white and green parts)

3/4 cup chicken broth

2 tablespoons soy sauce

1 tablespoon creamy peanut butter

2 teaspoons dark sesame oil

1 teaspoon hot sauce

1 teaspoon minced fresh ginger

1/4 cup coarsely chopped dry-roasted salted peanuts

Red Potato Salad with Bacon and Fresh Herbs

2 pounds small red potatoes
(8 to 10)

8 strips bacon

¼ cup minced red onion

½ cup mayonnaise

2 tablespoons red wine vinegar

2 tablespoons chopped fresh
parsley

1 tablespoon chopped fresh
rosemary

1 tablespoon chopped fresh basil

½ teaspoon salt

¼ teaspoon freshly ground
black pepper

SERVES 6

PACKING: Store in a sealable plastic container in the refrigerator until you're ready to pack it into a cold cooler.

Place the potatoes and water to cover in a large saucepan. Set over high heat and bring to a boil. Reduce the heat to medium and simmer for 20 minutes, until the potatoes are fork-tender. Drain. When the potatoes are cool enough to handle, cut them into quarters.

Meanwhile, cook the bacon in a hot skillet or in the microwave until crisp. Drain on paper towels and break into small pieces.

Transfer the potatoes to a large bowl and add the bacon and onion.

In a medium bowl, whisk together the mayonnaise, vinegar, parsley, rosemary, basil, salt, and pepper. Add to the still-warm potatoes and toss to coat.

Smoked Salmon with Caper Sour Cream and Black Bread

1 cup sour cream

¹/₄ cup minced red onion

2 tablespoons drained capers

1 tablespoon chopped fresh dill

¹/₂ teaspoon Dijon mustard

¹/₄ teaspoon freshly ground black pepper

1 pound smoked salmon

1 loaf hearty black bread, cut into ¹/₂-inch-thick slices

1 lemon, cut into wedges

PACKING: Store the sour cream mixture in a sealable plastic container, and wrap the smoked salmon in plastic wrap. Store both in the refrigerator until you're ready to pack them into a cold cooler. Cut the bread into slices in advance and store in a resealable plastic bag.

In a small bowl, combine the sour cream, onion, capers, dill, mustard, and pepper. Mix well to combine. Serve the sour cream mixture with the smoked salmon, black bread, and lemon wedges on the side.

Coriander Peanut Sauce with Crudités

SERVES 6 TO 8

PACKING: Store the sauce and the vegetables in separate sealable plastic containers in the refrigerator until you're ready to pack them into a cold cooler.

In a medium bowl, whisk together the sour cream, peanut butter, soy sauce, sesame oil, and coriander. Serve with the vegetables on the side.

FOR THE SAUCE

2 cups sour cream

4 tablespoons creamy peanut butter

2 tablespoons soy sauce

4 teaspoons dark sesame oil

$1/2$ teaspoon ground coriander

FOR THE CRUDITÉS

1 zucchini, cut into thin strips

1 yellow squash, cut into thin strips

2 green bell peppers, cored, seeded, and cut into thin strips

2 red bell peppers, cored, seeded, and cut into thin strips

4 cups fresh broccoli florets

2 cups cherry tomatoes

1 cup baby carrots

Mini Crab Cakes with Wasabi Mayonnaise

SERVES 4 TO 6

PACKING: Store the crab cakes and the wasabi mayonnaise in separate sealable plastic containers in the refrigerator until you're ready to pack them into a cold cooler.

Preheat the oven to 400°F.

In a large bowl, combine the crabmeat, sour cream, bread crumbs, mustard, Old Bay seasoning, oregano, and pepper. Mix gently, being careful not to break up the crabmeat.

Shape the mixture into 12 cakes, each about 1 inch thick and 1 inch wide. Place the flour in a shallow dish, add the crab cakes, and turn to coat both sides.

Heat the oil in a large ovenproof skillet over medium-high heat. Add the crab cakes and sauté 2 to 3 minutes per side, until golden brown. (To avoid crowding, sauté the crab cakes in batches.) Transfer the pan to the oven and bake for 15 to 20 minutes, until the crab cakes are cooked through.

Meanwhile, in a small bowl, whisk together the mayonnaise and wasabi paste.

Serve the crab cakes with the wasabi mayonnaise on the side.

FOR THE CRAB CAKES

1½ pounds lump crabmeat, picked over for shells

1 cup sour cream

¼ cup seasoned dry bread crumbs

2 teaspoons Dijon mustard

1 teaspoon Old Bay seasoning

1 teaspoon dried oregano

¼ teaspoon freshly ground black pepper

½ cup all-purpose flour

1 tablespoon olive or vegetable oil

FOR THE WASABI MAYONNAISE

½ cup mayonnaise

1 teaspoon wasabi paste, or more to taste

Minty Cucumber Salad

2 large cucumbers, peeled, halved, and seeded

1/4 cup chopped fresh mint

2 tablespoons chopped fresh parsley

1/2 cup plain yogurt

1 tablespoon red wine vinegar

1 tablespoon sugar

Salt and freshly ground black pepper

SERVES 4

PACKING: Store in a sealable plastic container in the refrigerator until you're ready to pack it into a cold cooler.

Cut the cucumbers crosswise into 1/4-inch-thick slices. Transfer them to a large bowl and add the mint and parsley. Toss to combine.

In a small bowl, whisk together the yogurt, vinegar, and sugar. Add to the cucumbers and toss to coat. Season to taste with salt and pepper.

PICNIC FACTOID

The word picnic comes from two French words, piquer, "to pick," and nique, "a morsel."

Mango Salad with Tomatoes and Red Onion

PACKING: Store in a sealable plastic container in the refrigerator until you're ready to pack it into a cold cooler.

In a medium bowl, combine the mangoes, tomatoes, onion, and cilantro. Toss to combine.

In a small bowl, whisk together the oil, lime juice, vinegar, and sugar. Add to the mango mixture and toss to combine. Season to taste with salt and pepper.

2 ripe mangoes, peeled, pitted, and cubed

2 yellow or red tomatoes, seeded and diced

1/4 cup minced red onion

2 tablespoons chopped fresh cilantro

1 tablespoon olive oil

1 tablespoon fresh lime juice

2 teaspoons balsamic vinegar

1 teaspoon sugar

Salt and freshly ground black pepper

TWO

wrapture and distinctive sandwiches

- ❖ Tangy Tuna and Sun-Dried Tomato Wrap in a Spinach Tortilla

- ❖ Roasted Red Pepper Wrap with Mozzarella and Basil Pesto

- ❖ Smoked Turkey Wrap with Brie and Granny Smiths

- ❖ Smoked Salmon Wrap with Chèvre, Red Onion, and Lemon

- ❖ Turkey Bacon, Watercress, and Tomato with Lime Mayonnaise on Toast

- ❖ Honey Ham Wrap with Gruyère, Endive, and Coarse Mustard

- ❖ Roast Beef Wrap with Asian Slaw and Swiss

- ❖ Soft-Shell Crab Sandwiches with Almond Mayonnaise

- ❖ Vegetarian Pita Pockets with Hummus, Marinated Eggplant, and Baby Greens

- ❖ Chilled Meat Loaf Sandwiches with Spicy Ketchup

- ❖ Prosciutto with Gorgonzola on Raisin Bread

- ❖ Grilled Chicken and Swiss with Pesto on Sourdough

Tangy Tuna and Sun-Dried Tomato Wrap in a Spinach Tortilla

SERVES 4

2 6-ounce cans white tuna in water, drained

¼ cup minced oil-packed sun-dried tomatoes

¼ cup mayonnaise

2 tablespoons chopped fresh parsley

1 tablespoon pickle relish

Salt and freshly ground black pepper

4 8-inch spinach or flour tortillas

4 red lettuce leaves

PACKING: Individually wrap each sandwich in plastic wrap and refrigerate until you're ready to pack them into a cold cooler.

In a medium bowl, combine the tuna, sun-dried tomatoes, mayonnaise, parsley, and relish. Mix well to combine. Season to taste with salt and pepper. Spoon a quarter of the tuna mixture onto each tortilla and spread to within ¼ inch of the edges. Place a lettuce leaf on top of the tuna on each tortilla and roll up tightly.

Roasted Red Pepper Wrap with Mozzarella and Basil Pesto

SERVES 4

PACKING: Individually wrap each sandwich in plastic wrap and refrigerate until you're ready to pack them into a cold cooler.

Spread 2 tablespoons of the pesto on one side of each tortilla to within ¼ inch of the edges. Top with the mozzarella, red peppers, and romaine. Sprinkle with black pepper and roll up tightly.

8 tablespoons prepared basil pesto (or see recipe on page 57)

4 8-inch flour or whole-wheat tortillas

8 ounces mozzarella cheese, thinly sliced

4 roasted red peppers (from water-packed jar), thinly sliced

1 cup shredded romaine lettuce

Freshly ground black pepper to taste

Smoked Turkey Wrap with Brie and Granny Smiths

8 tablespoons Brie

4 8-inch whole-wheat tortillas

2 Granny Smith apples,
cored and thinly sliced

12 ounces thinly sliced smoked
turkey breast

$1/2$ cup fresh watercress leaves

SERVES 4

PACKING: Individually wrap each sandwich in plastic wrap and refrigerate until you're ready to pack them into a cold cooler.

Spread 2 tablespoons of the Brie on one side of each tortilla to within $1/4$ inch of the edges. Top with the apple slices, smoked turkey, and watercress. Roll up tightly.

NOTE: IF YOU'RE NOT A BIG FAN OF BRIE, SUBSTITUTE CREAMY GOAT CHEESE, GOAT CHEESE WITH HERBS, CREAM CHEESE, OR EVEN VEGETABLE CREAM CHEESE. FOR VARIETY, TRY SUN-DRIED TOMATO TORTILLAS, BASIL TORTILLAS, OR POCKETLESS PITAS INSTEAD OF WHOLE-WHEAT TORTILLAS.

Smoked Salmon Wrap with Chèvre, Red Onion, and Lemon

PACKING: Individually wrap each sandwich in plastic wrap and refrigerate until you're ready to pack them into a cold cooler.

Spread 2 tablespoons of the chèvre on one side of each tortilla to within 1/4 inch of the edges. Top with the salmon, red onion, and dill. Squeeze lemon juice over the top and sprinkle with pepper to taste. Roll up tightly.

8 tablespoons soft mild chèvre
(goat's milk cheese),
such as Montrachet

4 8-inch whole-wheat
or flour tortillas

8 ounces smoked salmon

1/4 cup thinly sliced red onion

2 teaspoons chopped fresh dill

2 teaspoons fresh lemon juice

Freshly ground pepper

Turkey Bacon, Watercress, and Tomato with Lime Mayonnaise on Toast

16 strips turkey bacon

4 tablespoons mayonnaise

2 teaspoons fresh lime juice

$1/2$ teaspoon finely grated lime zest

Salt and freshly ground black pepper

8 slices whole-wheat bread, lightly toasted

1 beefsteak tomato, thinly sliced

1 cup fresh watercress leaves, well rinsed and dried

SERVES 4

PACKING: Individually wrap each sandwich in plastic wrap and refrigerate until you're ready to pack them into a cold cooler.

Cook the bacon in a hot skillet or in the microwave until crisp. Drain on paper towels.

Meanwhile, in a small bowl, combine the mayonnaise, lime juice, and lime zest. Season to taste with salt and pepper. Spread on half the toasted bread slices and top with the bacon, tomato, and watercress. Top with the remaining slices of bread.

Honey Ham Wrap with Gruyère, Endive, and Coarse Mustard

SERVES 4

PACKING: Individually wrap each sandwich in plastic wrap and refrigerate until you're ready to pack them into a cold cooler.

In a small bowl, whisk together the mustard and honey. Spread on one side of each tortilla to within $1/4$ inch of the edges. Top each tortilla with evenly divided amounts of the ham, Gruyère, and endive leaves. Roll up tightly.

2 tablespoons coarse mustard

1 tablespoon honey

4 8-inch whole-wheat or flour tortillas

12 ounces thinly sliced baked ham

8 ounces thinly sliced Gruyère cheese

1 cup fresh endive leaves

Roast Beef Wrap with Asian Slaw and Swiss

PACKING: Individually wrap each sandwich in plastic wrap and refrigerate until you're ready to pack them into a cold cooler.

In a small bowl, combine the cabbage, carrot, scallions, mayonnaise, and sesame oil. Toss to combine. Season to taste with salt and pepper.

    Spoon the cabbage mixture onto each tortilla and spread to within 1/2 inch of the edges. Top with roast beef and Swiss cheese, and roll up tightly.

1 cup shredded green cabbage

2 tablespoons shredded carrot

2 tablespoons chopped scallions (white and green parts)

1/4 cup mayonnaise

2 teaspoons dark sesame oil

Salt and freshly ground black pepper

4 8-inch flour tortillas

12 ounces thinly sliced roast beef

4 ounces thinly sliced Swiss cheese

Soft-Shell Crab Sandwiches with Almond Mayonnaise

FOR THE CRABS

1/3 cup all-purpose flour

1 teaspoon Old Bay seasoning

4 to 8 soft-shell crabs
(1 to 2 crabs per person,
depending on size)

2 tablespoons (1/4 stick)
unsalted butter

FOR THE MAYONNAISE AND SANDWICHES

6 tablespoons mayonnaise

2 tablespoons lightly toasted
slivered almonds (see Note)

1 tablespoon chopped
fresh parsley

Salt and freshly ground
black pepper

4 kaiser rolls, halved

SERVES 4

PACKING: Individually wrap each sandwich in plastic wrap and refrigerate until you're ready to pack them into a cold cooler.

In a shallow dish, combine the flour and Old Bay seasoning. Mix well with a fork to combine. Add the crabs and turn to coat. In a large skillet, melt the butter over medium-high heat. Shake off the excess flour from the crabs and add them to the hot butter. Cook for 5 minutes, until crisp and reddish brown, turning frequently with tongs.

Meanwhile, in a blender or food processor, combine the mayonnaise, almonds, and parsley. Purée until blended. Season to taste with salt and pepper.

Spread the mayonnaise mixture on the bottom halves of the rolls, add 1 or 2 soft-shell crabs, and cover with the top halves of the rolls.

NOTE: TOAST THE ALMONDS BY HEATING IN A SMALL SKILLET OVER MEDIUM HEAT UNTIL GOLDEN, SHAKING THE PAN FREQUENTLY; IT SHOULD TAKE ABOUT 3 TO 5 MINUTES.

Vegetarian Pita Pockets with Hummus, Marinated Eggplant, and Baby Greens

PACKING: Individually wrap each sandwich in plastic wrap and refrigerate until you're ready to pack them into a cold cooler.

Spread the hummus inside the pita pockets. Stuff with evenly divided amounts of the red peppers, eggplant, and baby greens.

NOTE: IF YOU CAN'T FIND MARINATED EGGPLANT IN YOUR MARKET'S DELI CASE, JUST USE PAN-SEARED EGGPLANT SLICES. TO MAKE THEM, SLICE ONE MEDIUM EGGPLANT INTO 1/4-INCH-THICK SLICES AND SAUTÉ FOR 2 MINUTES PER SIDE IN A SMALL AMOUNT OF OLIVE OIL. SEASON WITH SALT AND PEPPER AND USE AS DIRECTED ABOVE.

1 cup prepared hummus
(or see recipe on page 56)

4 whole-wheat or oat bran pita pockets, halved

2 cups thinly sliced roasted red peppers

2 cups sliced marinated eggplant (see Note)

1 cup mixed baby greens

Chilled Meat Loaf Sandwiches with Spicy Ketchup

FOR THE MEAT LOAF

Cooking spray

$1^{1}/_{2}$ pounds ground sirloin or lean ground beef

$^{1}/_{2}$ cup minced onion

$^{1}/_{2}$ cup seasoned dry bread crumbs

$^{1}/_{4}$ cup chopped fresh parsley

1 teaspoon dried oregano

1 large egg, beaten

$^{1}/_{2}$ teaspoon salt

$^{1}/_{4}$ teaspoon freshly ground black pepper

FOR THE KETCHUP AND SANDWICH

$^{1}/_{2}$ cup ketchup

2 teaspoons prepared horseradish

$^{1}/_{4}$ teaspoon hot sauce

16 to 20 slices hearty bread

PACKING: Individually wrap each sandwich in plastic wrap and refrigerate until you're ready to pack them into a cold cooler.

Preheat the oven to 375°F. and coat an 8-inch loaf pan with cooking spray.

In a large bowl, combine the beef, onion, bread crumbs, parsley, oregano, egg, salt, and pepper. Mix until well blended and press into the prepared loaf pan.

Bake for 60 minutes, until the top is golden and the loaf has pulled slightly away from the sides of the pan. Let stand for 10 minutes. Remove from the pan, wrap in plastic, and refrigerate until ready to serve.

Meanwhile, in a small bowl, combine the ketchup, horseradish, and hot sauce. Mix well.

To make the sandwiches, cut the chilled meat loaf into $^{1}/_{2}$- to 1-inch-thick slices. Spread the ketchup on half the bread slices and top with the meat loaf slices. Top with the remaining slices of bread.

Prosciutto with Gorgonzola on Raisin Bread

4 tablespoons mayonnaise

**1 tablespoon crumbled
Gorgonzola cheese**

**Salt and freshly ground
black pepper**

8 slices raisin bread

12 ounces thinly sliced prosciutto

1 cup baby spinach leaves

SERVES 4

PACKING: Individually wrap each sandwich in plastic wrap and refrigerate until you're ready to pack them into a cold cooler.

In a small bowl, combine the mayonnaise and Gorgonzola. Mix until blended. Season to taste with salt and pepper. Spread on half the bread slices and top with prosciutto and baby spinach leaves. Top with the remaining slices of bread.

Grilled Chicken and Swiss with Pesto on Sourdough

SERVES 4

PACKING: Individually wrap each sandwich in plastic wrap and refrigerate until you're ready to pack them into a cold cooler.

Preheat the outdoor grill, stovetop grill pan, or broiler. Brush both sides of the chicken with liquid smoke and season to taste with salt and pepper. Grill or broil for 3 to 5 minutes per side, until cooked through.

Spread the pesto on half the bread slices and top with grilled chicken, tomato, and Swiss cheese. Top with the remaining slices of bread.

4 skinless, boneless chicken breast halves

2 teaspoons liquid smoke

Salt and freshly ground black pepper

8 tablespoons prepared basil pesto (or see recipe on page 57)

8 thick slices sourdough bread

1 beefsteak tomato, thinly sliced

8 ounces thinly sliced Swiss cheese

THREE

extraordinary salads

- Lentil Salad with Carrots, Yellow Tomatoes, and Bell Peppers

- Garden-Fresh Tortellini Salad

- Spicy Sesame Noodles

- Pasta Spirals with Roasted Cherry Tomatoes and Goat Cheese

- Couscous Salad with Peas and Pearl Onions

- Chicken Salad with Raspberries and Walnuts

- Curried Crabmeat Salad

- Lobster-Papaya Salad with Chive Aïoli

- Sesame-Glazed Shrimp Salad with Sugar Snap Peas

- White Bean and Ham Salad with Avocado and Lemon Vinaigrette

- Marinated Italian Vegetable Salad with Olives

Lentil Salad with Carrots, Yellow Tomatoes, and Bell Peppers

SERVES 4

¹/₂ pound lentils, rinsed and picked over to remove any debris

2 bay leaves

2 garlic cloves, minced

1 yellow bell pepper, cored, seeded, and diced

1 red bell pepper, cored, seeded, and diced

¹/₂ cup diced carrots

¹/₂ cup chopped yellow or beefsteak tomatoes

8 pitted Greek (kalamata) olives, thinly sliced

¹/₄ cup diced red onion

¹/₄ cup chopped fresh parsley

¹/₄ cup red wine vinegar

2 tablespoons olive oil

¹/₂ teaspoon salt

¹/₄ teaspoon freshly ground black pepper

PACKING: Store in a sealable plastic container in the refrigerator until you're ready to pack it into a cold cooler.

In a large saucepan, combine the lentils, bay leaves, garlic, and water to cover. Set over high heat and bring to a boil. Reduce the heat to medium-low, cover, and simmer for 30 to 40 minutes, until the lentils are tender. Drain, and discard the bay leaves.

Transfer the lentils and garlic to a large bowl and add the bell peppers, carrots, tomatoes, olives, onion, and parsley. Toss to combine.

In a small bowl, whisk together the vinegar, oil, salt, and pepper. Pour over the lentil mixture and toss to combine.

Garden-Fresh Tortellini Salad

PACKING: Store the tortellini salad in a sealable plastic container in the refrigerator until you're ready to pack it into a cold cooler. Top with the Parmesan just before serving.

Cook the tortellini according to package directions. Drain and transfer to a large bowl. Add the zucchini, squash, bell pepper, scallions, and basil and toss to combine.

In a small bowl, whisk together the oil, vinegar, and mustard. Add to the tortellini and toss to coat. Season to taste with salt and pepper. Top with the Parmesan just before serving.

½ pound spinach tortellini

½ pound cheese tortellini

1 cup diced zucchini

1 cup diced yellow squash

1 red bell pepper, cored, seeded, and diced

2 scallions (white and green parts), chopped

¼ cup chopped fresh basil

4 tablespoons olive oil

2 tablespoons balsamic vinegar

2 teaspoons Dijon mustard

Salt and freshly ground black pepper

¼ cup grated Parmesan cheese

Spicy Sesame Noodles

PACKING: Store in a sealable plastic container in the refrigerator until you're ready to pack them into a cold cooler.

Cook the noodles according to package directions, adding the broccoli for the last 30 seconds of cooking time. Drain, rinse under cold water to prevent further cooking, and drain again.

Transfer the noodles and broccoli to a large bowl. Add the peanut oil, sesame oil, soy sauce, hot sauce, and red pepper flakes and toss to combine. Stir in the scallions and carrots. Season to taste with salt and pepper.

NOTE: FOR ADDED CRUNCH, TOP THE SALAD WITH DRY-ROASTED PEANUTS JUST BEFORE SERVING.

1 pound uncooked soba noodles
or whole-wheat spaghetti

2 cups fresh broccoli florets

2 tablespoons peanut oil

1 tablespoon dark sesame oil

1 tablespoon soy sauce

1 teaspoon hot sauce,
or more to taste

$1/2$ teaspoon crushed red
pepper flakes

$1/2$ cup chopped scallions
(white and green parts)

$1/2$ cup shredded carrots

Salt and freshly ground
black pepper

Pasta Spirals with Roasted Cherry Tomatoes and Goat Cheese

Cooking spray

1 pint cherry or grape tomatoes, halved

$1/2$ teaspoon salt, plus more to taste

1 pound uncooked rotelle or fusilli
(or any spiral-shaped pasta)

2 tablespoons balsamic vinegar

2 tablespoons olive oil

$1/4$ cup chopped fresh basil

Freshly ground black pepper

$1/4$ cup crumbled goat cheese

PACKING: Store the pasta in a sealable plastic container in the refrigerator until you're ready to pack it into a cold cooler. Top with the goat cheese just before serving.

Preheat the oven to 400°F. and coat a large baking sheet with cooking spray.

Spread the tomatoes on the prepared baking sheet, cut-side up, and sprinkle with $1/2$ teaspoon salt. Roast for 25 minutes, until browned and slightly shriveled.

Meanwhile, cook the pasta according to package directions. Drain and transfer to a large bowl. Add the vinegar and oil and toss to coat. Add the roasted tomatoes and basil and toss to combine. Season to taste with salt and pepper. Top with the goat cheese just before serving.

Couscous Salad with Peas and Pearl Onions

PACKING: Store in a sealable plastic container in the refrigerator until you're ready to pack it into a cold cooler.

In a medium saucepan, bring the chicken broth to a boil over high heat. Add the couscous and return to a boil, stirring constantly. Remove the pan from the heat and stir in the onions and peas. Cover and let stand for 5 minutes, until the liquid is absorbed. Transfer to a large bowl and add the dill and pimiento. Toss to combine.

In a small bowl, whisk together the vinegar, oil, and mustard. Add to the couscous and toss to combine. Season to taste with salt and pepper.

1½ cups chicken
or vegetable broth

1 cup whole-wheat
or regular couscous

1 10-ounce package frozen pearl
onions, thawed

½ cup frozen green peas,
thawed

2 tablespoons chopped fresh dill

2 tablespoons minced pimiento

2 tablespoons red or
white wine vinegar

2 tablespoons olive oil

1 teaspoon Dijon mustard

Salt and freshly ground
black pepper

PICNIC FACTOID

People have been enjoying picnics since the late seventeenth century, when the French word pique-nique first appeared. The word referred to a social gathering where each guest brought part of the meal (usually little nibbles). Later, picnics became an outdoor excursion to the country, where friends met to share a feast.

Chicken Salad with Raspberries and Walnuts

SERVES 4

PACKING: Store the salad in a sealable plastic container in the refrigerator until you're ready to pack it into a cold cooler. Top with the walnuts just before serving.

Place the chicken in a medium saucepan with water to cover. Set over high heat and bring to a boil. Reduce the heat to medium and simmer for 10 minutes, until the chicken is cooked through. Drain. When the chicken is cool enough to handle, cut it into 1-inch chunks.

Meanwhile, place the walnuts in a small skillet and set over medium-high heat. Cook for 2 to 3 minutes, until the nuts are golden brown, shaking the pan frequently. Set aside.

In a large bowl, combine the chicken, raspberries, and scallions. Toss gently to combine.

In a small bowl, whisk together the vinegar, oil, and mustard. Add to the chicken mixture and toss to coat. Season to taste with salt and pepper. Top with the toasted walnuts just before serving.

NOTE: TO SAVE TIME, BUY PRECOOKED ROASTED OR GRILLED CHICKEN BREASTS.

1 pound skinless, boneless chicken breasts

¼ cup chopped walnuts

1 cup fresh raspberries

2 scallions (white and green parts), chopped

1 tablespoon raspberry white wine vinegar

1 tablespoon olive oil

2 teaspoons Dijon mustard

Salt and freshly ground black pepper to taste

Curried Crabmeat Salad

1/4 cup mayonnaise

2 tablespoons minced pimiento

1 teaspoon curry powder

1/2 teaspoon ground coriander

1 pound fresh lump crabmeat, picked over for shells

2 tablespoons chopped fresh cilantro

Salt and freshly ground black pepper

SERVES 4

PACKING: Store in a sealable plastic container in the refrigerator until you're ready to pack it into a cold cooler.

In a medium bowl, combine the mayonnaise, pimiento, curry powder, and coriander. Mix well. Add the crab and cilantro and toss gently to coat. Season to taste with salt and pepper.

Lobster-Papaya Salad with Chive Aïoli

SERVES 4

PACKING: Store in a sealable plastic container in the refrigerator until you're ready to pack it into a cold cooler.

In a large bowl, combine the lobster, papaya, lime juice, and ginger. Toss to combine.

In a small bowl, whisk together the mayonnaise, chives, dill, and garlic powder. Add to the lobster mixture and toss to coat. Season to taste with salt and pepper.

1 pound cooked lobster tail meat

1 cup diced papaya

1 tablespoon fresh lime juice

1 teaspoon minced fresh ginger

1/4 cup mayonnaise

2 tablespoons chopped
fresh chives

1 tablespoon chopped fresh dill

1/2 teaspoon garlic powder

Salt and freshly ground
black pepper

Sesame-Glazed Shrimp Salad with Sugar Snap Peas

4 teaspoons sesame oil

1 pound raw medium shrimp, peeled and deveined

1 cup sugar snap peas, ends trimmed

¹⁄₄ cup mayonnaise

2 tablespoons chopped fresh cilantro

Salt and freshly ground black pepper

SERVES 4

PACKING: Store in a sealable plastic container in the refrigerator until you're ready to pack it into a cold cooler.

Heat 2 teaspoons of the oil in a large skillet over medium-high heat. Add the shrimp and cook for 3 to 5 minutes, until bright pink, turning frequently. Transfer the shrimp to a large bowl.

Meanwhile, blanch the snap peas in a large pot of boiling water for 30 seconds, until bright green and crisp-tender. Drain and set aside.

In a small bowl, whisk together the mayonnaise, cilantro, and the remaining 2 teaspoons of oil. Add to the shrimp and toss to coat. Add the snap peas and toss to combine. Season to taste with salt and pepper.

White Bean and Ham Salad with Avocado and Lemon Vinaigrette

2 15-ounce cans white beans
(Great Northern or cannellini),
rinsed and drained

12 ounces baked ham, diced

¼ cup minced red onion

¼ cup chopped fresh parsley

1 ripe Hass avocado, peeled,
pitted, and diced

4 tablespoons olive oil

2 tablespoons fresh lemon juice

2 teaspoons Dijon mustard

Salt and freshly ground
black pepper

SERVES 4

PACKING: Store in a sealable plastic container in the refrigerator until you're ready to pack it into a cold cooler.

In a large bowl, combine the beans, ham, onion, parsley, and avocado. Toss to combine.

In a small bowl, whisk together the oil, lemon juice, and mustard. Add to the bean mixture and toss to combine. Season to taste with salt and pepper.

Marinated Italian Vegetable Salad with Olives

PACKING: Store in a sealable plastic container in the refrigerator until you're ready to pack it into a cold cooler.

In a large bowl, combine the vinegar, garlic, and bay leaves. Set aside.

Bring a large pot of water to a boil. Add the cauliflower, carrots, and celery and cook for 1 minute. Drain and transfer the hot vegetables to the vinegar mixture. Add the artichoke hearts, olives, roasted red peppers, oil, and capers. Mix well. Cover and refrigerate for at least 24 hours (and up to 48 hours).

Drain the vegetables and remove the bay leaves. Season to taste with salt and pepper.

$3/4$ cup white wine vinegar

4 garlic cloves, peeled and halved

2 bay leaves

3 cups cauliflower florets

$1^1/2$ cups sliced carrots (cut into $^1/8$-inch-thick rounds)

2 celery stalks, chopped

1 14-ounce can artichoke hearts, drained and halved

$^1/2$ cup assorted pitted olives

$^1/2$ cup thinly sliced roasted red peppers (from water-packed jar)

2 tablespoons olive oil

1 tablespoon drained capers

Salt and freshly ground black pepper

FOUR

dips and spreads with toasts, twists, crisps, and other bread concoctions

- ❧ White Bean and Chickpea Hummus
- ❧ Creamy Basil Pesto Dip
- ❧ Tangy Roasted Red Pepper Dip
- ❧ Spicy Black Bean Dip
- ❧ Smoked Salmon Spread
- ❧ Roasted Garlic Spread with Goat Cheese
- ❧ Artichoke Dip with Parmesan
- ❧ Sweet-and-Hot Mango Chutney

- ❧ Sun-Dried Tomato Twists
- ❧ Walnut-Cheddar Crisps
- ❧ Parmesan Cheese Twists
- ❧ Cumin-Dusted Pita Wedges
- ❧ Zucchini Bread with Lemon
- ❧ Cheddar Corn Bread with Green Chilies
- ❧ Onion and Black Pepper Flatbread
- ❧ Garlic-Rosemary Focaccia

White Bean and Chickpea Hummus

1 15-ounce can chickpeas, rinsed
and drained

1 15-ounce can white beans
(Great Northern or cannellini),
rinsed and drained

$1/4$ cup sesame paste (tahini)

2 garlic cloves, minced

2 tablespoons fresh lemon juice

$1/2$ teaspoon ground cumin

Salt and freshly ground
black pepper

MAKES 2 CUPS

PACKING: Store in a sealable plastic container in the refrigerator until you're ready to pack it into a cold cooler.

In a food processor, combine the chickpeas, white beans, sesame paste, garlic, lemon juice, and cumin. Process until smooth. Season to taste with salt and pepper.

Creamy Basil Pesto Dip

PACKING: Store in a sealable plastic container in the refrigerator until you're ready to pack it into a cold cooler.

In a blender or food processor, combine the basil, sour cream, Parmesan, oil, pine nuts, garlic, and salt. Process until smooth.

NOTE: TOAST PINE NUTS BY HEATING IN A SMALL SKILLET OVER MEDIUM HEAT UNTIL GOLDEN, SHAKING THE PAN FREQUENTLY; IT SHOULD TAKE 3 TO 5 MINUTES.

FOR A CILANTRO VERSION, SUBSTITUTE AN EQUIVALENT AMOUNT OF FRESH CILANTRO LEAVES FOR THE BASIL.

1 cup packed fresh basil leaves (see Note)

$1/2$ cup sour cream

$1/4$ cup grated Parmesan cheese

3 tablespoons olive oil

2 tablespoons lightly toasted pine nuts (see Note)

2 garlic cloves, peeled

$1/2$ teaspoon salt

Tangy Roasted Red Pepper Dip

2 12-ounce jars water-packed roasted red peppers, undrained

2 garlic cloves, minced

1 tablespoon minced fresh ginger

2 teaspoons Dijon mustard

Salt and freshly ground black pepper

1 yellow bell pepper, cored, seeded, and diced

1 cup diced button mushrooms

¼ cup chopped fresh basil

MAKES 2 CUPS

PACKING: Store in a sealable plastic container in the refrigerator until you're ready to pack it into a cold cooler.

In a blender or food processor, combine the roasted red peppers, garlic, ginger, and mustard. Process until smooth. Season to taste with salt and pepper. Transfer the mixture to a large bowl and fold in the bell pepper, mushrooms, and basil.

Spicy Black Bean Dip

PACKING: Store in a sealable plastic container in the refrigerator until you're ready to pack it into a cold cooler.

In a food processor, combine the beans, sour cream, chipotle chile plus sauce, and cumin. Process until smooth. Transfer to a medium bowl and fold in the tomato, chilies, and cilantro.

2 15-ounce cans black beans, rinsed and drained

$1/2$ cup sour cream

1 minced chipotle chile in adobo, plus 1 teaspoon adobo sauce from can

$1/2$ teaspoon ground cumin

1 ripe beefsteak tomato, diced

1 4-ounce can chopped green chilies

2 tablespoons chopped fresh cilantro

PICNIC FACTOID

By the mid-1800s, picnicking had become a popular pastime in England, Australia, and the United States.

Smoked Salmon Spread

8 ounces cream cheese, softened

¼ cup heavy cream

1 tablespoon chopped fresh dill

1 teaspoon fresh lemon juice

⅛ teaspoon freshly ground black pepper

4 ounces smoked salmon, shredded or finely minced

2 scallions (green parts only), chopped

MAKES 2 CUPS

PACKING: Store the spread in a sealable plastic container in the refrigerator until you're ready to pack it into a cold cooler. Top with the scallions just before serving.

In the bowl of a standing mixer, combine the cream cheese and heavy cream. Mix on low speed until smooth. Beat in the dill, lemon juice, and pepper. Fold in the salmon. Sprinkle the scallions over the top just before serving.

Roasted Garlic Spread with Goat Cheese

MAKES 1¹/₂ CUPS

PACKING: Store the spread in a sealable plastic container in the refrigerator until you're ready to pack it into a cold cooler. Top with the parsley just before serving.

Preheat the oven to 400°F.

Slice off the top ¹/₄ inch of the garlic heads to reveal the cloves. Wrap the heads in foil and roast them for 45 minutes, until soft. Loosen the foil and let the garlic cool. When the cloves are cool enough to handle, squeeze them from their skins and transfer to a blender or food processor. Add the sour cream, goat cheese, and Parmesan and process until smooth. Season to taste with salt and pepper. Sprinkle the parsley over the top just before serving.

2 heads of garlic

1 cup sour cream

¹/₄ cup goat cheese

2 tablespoons grated Parmesan cheese

Salt and freshly ground black pepper

2 tablespoons chopped fresh parsley

Artichoke Dip with Parmesan

2 cups sour cream

6 tablespoons grated Parmesan
cheese

1 tablespoon Dijon mustard

1 teaspoon dried oregano

$1/4$ teaspoon freshly ground
black pepper

2 14-ounce cans artichoke hearts,
drained and cut into
$1/2$-inch pieces

2 tablespoons chopped
fresh parsley

2 tablespoons seasoned dry
bread crumbs

$1/2$ teaspoon paprika

MAKES 4 CUPS

PACKING: Store in a sealable plastic container in the refrigerator until
you're ready to pack it into a cold cooler.

Preheat the oven to 350°F.

In a large bowl, combine the sour cream, 4 tablespoons of the
Parmesan, the mustard, oregano, and pepper. Fold in the artichokes
and parsley. Transfer to a baking dish or ovenproof crock.

In a small bowl, combine the bread crumbs, the remaining
2 tablespoons of Parmesan, and the paprika. Sprinkle the bread-
crumb mixture over the sour-cream mixture and bake for 20 minutes, until the top is golden brown.

Sweet-and-Hot Mango Chutney

MAKES 2 CUPS

PACKING: Store in a sealable plastic container in the refrigerator until you're ready to pack it into a cold cooler.

In a medium saucepan, combine the mango, raisins, onion, chili pepper, vinegar, and brown sugar with 2 tablespoons of water. Set over medium-high heat and simmer for 5 to 10 minutes, until the mango breaks down and the mixture becomes thick.

2 cups diced fresh mango

1/2 cup raisins

1/4 cup minced red onion

1 habanero chili pepper, seeded and minced

2 tablespoons cider vinegar

1 tablespoon light brown sugar

Sun-Dried Tomato Twists

1 sheet frozen puff pastry, thawed according to package directions

1/4 cup prepared sun-dried tomato pesto

1/4 cup finely grated sharp Cheddar cheese

PACKING: Store in resealable plastic bags.

Preheat the oven to 400°F.

Roll out the puff pastry into a rectangle about 12 × 15 inches. Spread the pesto evenly over the dough, to within 1/8 inch of the edges.

Fold the dough in half lengthwise. Roll out again into a 12 × 15-inch rectangle. Sprinkle the Cheddar over the new rectangle.

Using a sharp knife, cut the dough crosswise into 1/2-inch-thick strips. Take each strip by the ends and twist into a corkscrew. Arrange the twists on a large baking sheet and press down the ends.

Bake for 10 minutes, until puffed up and golden brown. Cool completely before packing.

Walnut-Cheddar Crisps

PACKING: Store in resealable plastic bags.

Preheat the oven to 350°F. and coat a large baking sheet with cooking spray.

In the bowl of a standing mixer, beat together the butter and Cheddar until smooth. Mixing on low speed, beat in the flour, walnuts, egg yolk, salt, and cayenne.

Drop the dough by rounded teaspoons onto the prepared baking sheet 3 inches apart. Flatten each into a 1½-inch-wide round. Bake for 15 to 18 minutes, until golden around the edges. Cool completely on wire racks before packing.

Cooking spray

½ cup (1 stick) unsalted butter, softened

8 ounces coarsely grated sharp Cheddar cheese

⅔ cup all-purpose flour

⅔ cup finely chopped walnuts

1 large egg yolk

½ teaspoon salt

½ teaspoon cayenne

Parmesan Cheese Twists

1 sheet frozen puff pastry, thawed according to package directions

1/2 cup grated Parmesan cheese (see Note)

PACKING: Store in resealable plastic bags.

Preheat the oven to 400°F.

Roll out the puff pastry into a rectangle about 12 × 15 inches. Sprinkle half of the Parmesan evenly over the dough and press the cheese into the dough with a rolling pin.

Fold the dough in half lengthwise. Roll out again into a 12 × 15-inch rectangle. Sprinkle the remaining cheese over the new rectangle.

Using a sharp knife, cut the dough crosswise into 1/2-inch-thick strips. Take each strip by the ends and twist into a corkscrew. Arrange the twists on a large baking sheet and press down the ends.

Bake for 10 minutes, until puffed up and golden brown. Cool completely before packing.

NOTE: FOR THE BEST FLAVOR, USE A GOOD-QUALITY PARMESAN CHEESE.

Also pictured: Onion and Black Pepper Flatbread (page 72) and Sun-Dried Tomato Twists (page 64).

Cumin-Dusted Pita Wedges

MAKES 32 WEDGES

Cooking spray

8 pita pockets

1 to 2 teaspoons ground cumin

Salt and freshly ground
black pepper to taste

PACKING: Store in resealable plastic bags.

Preheat the oven to 400°F. and coat a large baking sheet with cooking spray.

Cut each pita pocket into 4 wedges. Transfer to the prepared baking sheet and sprinkle on the cumin and salt and pepper. Bake for 8 to 10 minutes, until golden brown. Cool completely before packing.

Zucchini Bread with Lemon

SERVES 8 TO 10

PACKING: Wrap in plastic wrap. Slice just before serving.

Preheat the oven to 350°F. and coat an 8-inch loaf pan with cooking spray.

In a large bowl, combine the flour, sugar, baking powder, cinnamon, baking soda, and salt. Mix well with a fork, make a well in the center, and set aside.

In a medium bowl, whisk together the buttermilk, oil, eggs, and lemon juice. Stir in the zucchini and lemon zest. Add to the well in the dry ingredients and mix until just blended.

Pour the batter into the prepared pan and bake for 55 to 60 minutes, until a toothpick inserted near the center comes out clean. Cool in the pan on a wire rack for 10 minutes. Remove from the pan and cool completely. Slice just before serving.

Cooking spray

3 cups all-purpose flour

3/4 cup sugar

4 teaspoons baking powder

1 teaspoon ground cinnamon

1/2 teaspoon baking soda

1/2 teaspoon salt

1 cup buttermilk

4 tablespoons corn oil

2 large eggs

2 tablespoons fresh lemon juice

1 cup coarsely shredded zucchini

2 teaspoons finely grated lemon zest

Cheddar Corn Bread with Green Chilies

PACKING: Wrap in plastic wrap. Cut into squares just before serving.

Preheat the oven to 400°F. and coat an 8-inch-square baking pan with cooking spray.

In a large bowl, combine the cornmeal, flour, baking powder, salt, baking soda, and cayenne. Mix well with a fork, make a well in the center, and set aside.

In a medium bowl, whisk together the milk, egg, and oil. Stir in the corn, Cheddar, and chilies. Fold the milk mixture into the well in the dry ingredients and mix until just blended.

Pour the batter into the prepared pan and bake for 20 minutes, until a toothpick inserted near the center comes out clean. Cool in the pan on a wire rack for 10 minutes. Remove from the pan and cool completely. Cut into squares just before serving.

Cooking spray

1 cup yellow cornmeal

1 cup all-purpose flour

2 teaspoons baking powder

1 teaspoon salt

1/2 teaspoon baking soda

1/4 teaspoon cayenne

1 cup whole milk

1 large egg

2 tablespoons corn oil

1 14-ounce can whole kernel corn, drained

1/2 cup grated sharp Cheddar cheese

1 4-ounce can chopped green chilies

Also pictured: Sweet-and-Hot Mango Chutney (page 63).

Onion and Black Pepper Flatbread

Cooking spray

2 tablespoons plus 4 teaspoons
olive oil

1 1/4 cups chopped onion

1 cup warm water (about 110°F.)

1 packet fast-acting yeast

1 teaspoon coarsely ground
black pepper

1 teaspoon salt, preferably
coarse sea salt

2 1/2 cups all-purpose flour

SERVES 6 TO 8

PACKING: Store in resealable plastic bags. Slice into wedges just before serving.

Preheat the oven to 500°F. and coat two large baking sheets with cooking spray.

Heat 1 tablespoon of the oil in a large skillet over medium-high heat. Add 1 cup of the onion and cook for 3 minutes, until soft. Set aside.

Place the warm water in a large mixing bowl and sprinkle in the yeast. Add 1 tablespoon of the oil, 3/4 teaspoon of the black pepper, and 1/2 teaspoon of the salt. Add the cooked onion and 1 cup of the flour and mix well. Add the remaining flour and mix with a dough hook (or your hands) until a manageable dough forms.

Transfer the dough to a lightly floured surface and knead it for 15 seconds. Quarter the dough and form each piece into a 1/4-inch-thick round. Transfer the rounds to the prepared baking sheets and, using a finger, press indentations into the dough at 1-inch intervals.

Drizzle the remaining 4 teaspoons of olive oil over the rounds and top with the remaining 1/4 cup of the onion, the remaining 1/4 teaspoon of black pepper, and the remaining 1/2 teaspoon of salt. Bake for 15 to 18 minutes, until golden brown. Cool completely before packing.

Garlic-Rosemary Focaccia

SERVES 6 TO 8

PACKING: Wrap in plastic wrap. Slice just before serving.

Preheat the oven to 400°F. and coat an 11 × 7-inch baking pan with cooking spray.

Punch down the dough with your fist and press it into the bottom of the prepared pan. Set aside.

Heat the oil in a large nonstick skillet over a medium flame. Add the onion, garlic, and sugar and sauté for 10 minutes, until the onions are tender and golden brown. Stir in the rosemary, salt, and pepper and heat through.

Top the dough with the onion mixture and sprinkle the top with the Parmesan. Bake for 20 to 25 minutes, until golden brown. Cool in the pan on a wire rack for 5 minutes. Remove from the pan and cool completely. Slice just before serving.

Cooking spray

1 pound frozen bread dough, thawed according to package directions

1 tablespoon olive oil

1 cup thinly sliced red onion

4 garlic cloves, minced

2 tablespoons sugar

2 tablespoons chopped fresh rosemary

1/2 teaspoon salt

1/4 teaspoon freshly ground black pepper

3 to 4 tablespoons grated Parmesan cheese

FIVE

sweet temptations

- Pecan Squares
- Toffee-Chocolate Bars with Cashews
- Chocolate-Dunked Coconut Macaroons
- Oatmeal Raisin Cookies
- Hazelnut Half-Moon Cookies
- Tropical Fruit Salad with Coconut

- Mini Chocolate Cakes
- Banana-Raspberry Bread
- Strawberry-Almond Scones
- Blueberry Corn Muffins
- Almond Biscotti
- Apple-Cinnamon Coffee Cake

Pecan Squares

Cooking spray

2 cups all-purpose flour

²/₃ cup confectioners' sugar

¹/₈ teaspoon salt

1 cup (2 sticks) unsalted butter, softened, plus 11 tablespoons unsalted butter, melted

1 cup packed light brown sugar

3 tablespoons heavy cream

3 cups coarsely chopped pecans

PACKING: Store in resealable plastic bags.

Preheat the oven to 350°F. and coat a 9 × 13-inch baking pan with cooking spray.

In a large bowl, combine the flour, confectioners' sugar, and salt. Add the softened butter and, using a fork, mix until fine crumbs form. Press the mixture into the bottom of the prepared pan. Bake for 20 minutes.

Meanwhile, make the topping: In a medium bowl, combine the melted butter with the brown sugar and heavy cream. Mix until well blended. Fold in the pecans. Pour this mixture over the crust, return the pan to the oven, and bake for 25 more minutes, until the top is almost set—it will set completely upon cooling. Cool in the pan on a wire rack before cutting into squares and packing.

Toffee-Chocolate Bars with Cashews

MAKES 24 BARS

PACKING: Wrap in plastic wrap or store in resealable plastic bags.

Preheat the oven to 350°F. and coat a 9 × 13-inch baking pan with cooking spray.

In the bowl of a standing mixer, combine the butter and sugar and beat until creamy. Beat the in egg yolk. Mixing on low speed, beat in the flour and vanilla. Pour the batter into the prepared pan and smooth the surface. Bake for 25 minutes.

Sprinkle the chocolate chips over the dough and bake for 3 to 4 more minutes, until the chocolate melts. Using the back of a spoon, smooth the melted chocolate evenly over the surface and sprinkle with the cashews. Cool in the pan on a wire rack before cutting into bars and packing.

Cooking spray

1 cup (2 sticks) unsalted butter, softened

1 cup packed light brown sugar

1 large egg yolk

2 cups all-purpose flour

1 teaspoon pure vanilla extract

12 ounces milk chocolate chips

1 cup chopped dry-roasted salted cashews

PICNIC FACTOID

Picnics were so popular in nineteenth-century France that French Impressionists Georges Seurat (A Sunday Afternoon on the Island of La Grande Jatte) and Edouard Manet (Le Déjeuner sur l'herbe) immortalized picnics in their paintings.

Chocolate-Dunked Coconut Macaroons

Cooking spray

1/3 cup all-purpose flour,
plus more for dusting the
baking sheet

2 1/2 cups shredded coconut

1/8 teaspoon salt

2/3 cup sweetened
condensed milk

1 teaspoon pure vanilla extract

6 ounces semisweet
chocolate chips

MAKES 24 MACAROONS

PACKING: Store in resealable plastic bags.

Preheat the oven to 350°F. Coat a large baking sheet with cooking spray and dust it with flour.

In a large bowl, combine the flour, coconut, and salt. Mix well with a fork to combine. Add the condensed milk and vanilla and mix well.

Drop the batter by heaping tablespoons onto the prepared baking sheet 1 inch apart. Bake for 20 minutes, until golden brown. Cool on a wire rack for 10 minutes.

Meanwhile, melt the chocolate in a double boiler or in a bowl over simmering water. Dip the macaroons in the melted chocolate to coat one half. Return the cookies to the rack (or place on wax paper) and cool completely.

Oatmeal Raisin Cookies

Cooking spray

²/₃ cup all-purpose flour

1 teaspoon ground cinnamon

¹/₂ teaspoon baking powder

¹/₂ teaspoon baking soda

¹/₂ teaspoon salt

¹/₄ teaspoon freshly grated
nutmeg

12 tablespoons (1¹/₂ sticks)
unsalted butter or margarine,
softened

1 cup packed light brown sugar

¹/₂ cup granulated sugar

1 large egg

1 teaspoon pure vanilla extract

3 cups regular or quick-cooking
rolled oats

1 cup raisins

PACKING: Store in resealable plastic bags.

Preheat the oven to 350°F. and coat a large baking sheet with cooking spray.

In a medium bowl, combine the flour, cinnamon, baking powder, baking soda, salt, and nutmeg. Mix well with a fork and set aside.

In a large mixing bowl, beat together the butter and both sugars until light and fluffy. Beat in the egg. Beat in 2 tablespoons of water and the vanilla. Gradually add the flour mixture and mix until blended. Fold in the oats and raisins.

Drop the batter by tablespoons onto the prepared baking sheet at least 1 inch apart. Bake for 10 to 12 minutes, until golden brown in the middle and slightly darker around the edges. Cool on the baking sheet for 5 minutes. Transfer to wire racks to cool completely.

Hazelnut Half-Moon Cookies

PACKING: Store in resealable plastic bags.

Preheat the oven to 350°F. and coat a large baking sheet with cooking spray.

In a food processor, combine the hazelnuts, flour, and salt. Process until the nuts are finely ground.

In the bowl of a standing mixer, beat together the butter and 1 cup of the confectioners' sugar until creamy. Beat in the vanilla and almond extracts. On low speed, gradually add the ground nut mixture and mix until blended.

Using your hands, shape 1 inch of dough into a half moon, or crescent. Repeat with the remaining dough. Place the cookies on the prepared baking sheet and bake for 15 minutes, until lightly golden.

Place the remaining $1/2$ cup of confectioners' sugar in a small, shallow bowl. While the cookies are still warm, toss them in the sugar to coat. Cool completely before packing.

Cooking spray

1 cup toasted skinned hazelnuts

2 cups all-purpose flour

$1/8$ teaspoon salt

1 cup (2 sticks) unsalted butter, softened

$1^1/2$ cups confectioners' sugar

2 teaspoons pure vanilla extract

$1/2$ teaspoon pure almond extract

Tropical Fruit Salad with Coconut

SERVES 4

PACKING: Store the salad in a sealable plastic container in the refrigerator until you're ready to pack it into a cold cooler. Add the coconut just before serving.

In a large bowl, combine the mango, papaya, bananas, orange juice, and lime juice. Stir in the coconut just before serving.

NOTE: TOAST THE COCONUT BY SPREADING IT OUT ON A BAKING SHEET AND BAKING AT 300°F. FOR 3 TO 5 MINUTES, UNTIL GOLDEN.

2 cups diced fresh mango

2 cups diced fresh papaya

2 bananas, sliced crosswise into $1/2$-inch-thick rounds

$1/2$ cup orange juice

1 tablespoon fresh lime juice

$1/4$ cup lightly toasted shredded coconut (see Note)

Mini Chocolate Cakes

Cooking spray

1³/₄ cups all-purpose flour

1³/₄ cups packed light
brown sugar

³/₄ cup cocoa powder

1¹/₂ teaspoons baking soda

1¹/₂ teaspoons baking powder

1¹/₄ cups milk

2 large eggs

4 tablespoons butter or
margarine, melted

1¹/₂ teaspoons pure
vanilla extract

1 cup boiling water

PACKING: Individually wrap cakes in plastic wrap and store at room temperature for up to 12 hours; refrigerate cakes if they will be sitting longer than 12 hours.

Preheat the oven to 350°F. and and coat a 9 × 12-inch baking pan with cooking spray.

In a large bowl, combine the flour, brown sugar, cocoa, baking soda, and baking powder. Mix well with a fork to break up the brown sugar and set aside.

In the bowl of a standing mixer, combine the milk, eggs, butter, and vanilla. Mix on low speed until blended. Gradually beat in the boiling water. Gradually add the flour mixture and mix on low speed until blended. Pour the batter unto the prepared pan and bake for 25 minutes, or until a toothpick inserted near the center comes out clean. Cool in the pan, on a wire rack, before cutting the cake into 12 equal squares.

Banana-Raspberry Bread

PACKING: Wrap in plastic wrap. Slice just before serving.

Preheat the oven to 350°F. and coat an 8-inch loaf pan with cooking spray.

In a medium bowl, combine the flour, sugar, baking powder, baking soda, and salt. Mix well with a fork and set aside.

In a large bowl or a food processor, mash the bananas until mushy. Add the milk, egg, and vanilla and mix or process until blended. Add the dry ingredients and mix or process until just blended. Fold in the raspberries.

Pour the batter into the prepared pan and bake for 1 hour, or until a toothpick inserted near the center comes out clean. Cool in the pan on a wire rack for 10 minutes. Remove from the pan and cool completely. Slice just before serving.

Cooking spray

2 cups all-purpose flour

$^3/_4$ cup sugar

2 teaspoons baking powder

$^1/_2$ teaspoon baking soda

$^1/_2$ teaspoon salt

4 large ripe or overripe bananas

$^1/_4$ cup whole milk

1 large egg

1 teaspoon pure vanilla extract

1 cup fresh or frozen raspberries (keep frozen until ready to use)

Strawberry-Almond Scones

SERVES 12

PACKING: Wrap in plastic wrap or store in resealable plastic bags.

Preheat the oven to 400°F. and coat a large baking sheet with cooking spray.

In a large bowl or a food processor, combine the flour, $1/3$ cup of the sugar, the baking powder, baking soda, and salt. Add the butter and mix together with your fingers or process until the mixture resembles coarse meal. Set aside.

In a medium bowl, whisk together the egg whites, buttermilk, and vanilla. Stir in the strawberry preserves and almonds. Fold into the dry ingredients and mix until just blended.

Transfer the dough to a lightly floured surface and knead five times. Place the dough on the prepared baking sheet and shape into a 9-inch circle. Using a sharp knife, make 12 cuts $1/4$ inch deep in a spoke pattern across the top. Sprinkle with the remaining tablespoon of sugar. Bake for 15 to 20 minutes, until golden and a knife inserted near the center comes out clean. Cool on a wire rack before slicing into 12 wedges.

Cooking spray

$2^3/4$ cups all-purpose flour

$1/3$ cup plus 1 tablespoon sugar

2 teaspoons baking powder

$1/2$ teaspoon baking soda

$1/4$ teaspoon salt

3 tablespoons unsalted butter, chilled and cut up

2 large egg whites

$1/4$ cup buttermilk

1 teaspoon pure vanilla extract

$2/3$ cup strawberry preserves

$1/3$ cup slivered almonds

Blueberry Corn Muffins

Cooking spray

1 cup yellow cornmeal

1 cup all-purpose flour

$1/3$ cup sugar

$2^1/2$ teaspoons baking powder

$1/4$ teaspoon salt

1 cup buttermilk

6 tablespoons ($3/4$ stick)
unsalted butter, melted

1 large egg

1 teaspoon pure vanilla extract

$1^2/3$ cups fresh or frozen
blueberries (keep frozen until
ready to use)

PACKING: Store in resealable plastic bags.

Preheat the oven to 400°F. and spray a muffin pan with cooking spray (or line muffin cups with paper liners).

In a large bowl, combine the cornmeal, flour, sugar, baking powder, and salt. Mix well with a fork, make a well in the center, and set aside.

In a medium bowl, whisk together the buttermilk, melted butter, egg, and vanilla. Add to the well in the dry ingredients and mix until just combined. Fold in the blueberries.

Spoon the batter into muffin cups until two-thirds full. Bake for 20 to 25 minutes, until a toothpick inserted into a center muffin comes out clean. Cool in the pan on a wire rack for 10 minutes. Remove from the pan and cool completely.

Almond Biscotti

PACKING: Store in resealable plastic bags.

Preheat the oven to 325°F. and coat a large baking sheet with cooking spray.

In a large bowl, combine the flour, sugar, almonds, baking soda, and salt. Mix well with a fork and set aside.

In a small bowl, whisk together the eggs and egg whites. Whisk in the milk and vanilla and almond extracts. Add to the dry ingredients and mix until a manageable dough forms.

Transfer the dough to a lightly floured surface and shape into a 10-inch log. Place on the prepared baking sheet and bake for 30 to 35 minutes, until a knife inserted near the center comes out clean. Reduce the oven temperature to 300°F.

Cut the log crosswise into 18 slices and return them to the baking sheet. Bake for 20 more minutes, turning once, until golden. Cool completely before packing.

Cooking spray

2 cups all-purpose flour

$2/3$ cup sugar

$1/3$ cup slivered almonds

$3/4$ teaspoon baking soda

$1/4$ teaspoon salt

2 large eggs

2 large egg whites

$1/4$ cup whole milk

1 teaspoon pure vanilla extract

1 teaspoon pure almond extract

Apple-Cinnamon Coffee Cake

Cooking spray

1½ cups all-purpose flour

1 cup plus 2 tablespoons sugar

1½ teaspoons baking powder

1½ teaspoons ground cinnamon

½ teaspoon salt

1 cup chunky applesauce

½ cup whole milk

2 tablespoons (¼ stick) unsalted butter, melted

1 large egg

1 teaspoon pure vanilla extract

2 tablespoons chopped walnuts

SERVES 8

PACKING: Wrap in plastic wrap. Slice just before serving.

Preheat the oven to 350°F. and coat an 8-inch square or round cake pan with cooking spray.

In a large bowl, combine the flour, 1 cup of the sugar, the baking powder, 1 teaspoon of the cinnamon, and the salt. Mix well with a fork, make a well in the center, and set aside.

In a medium bowl, whisk together the applesauce, milk, butter, egg, and vanilla. Fold into the well in the dry ingredients until just blended. Pour the batter into the prepared pan and bake for 45 minutes, until a toothpick inserted near the center comes out clean.

Meanwhile, make the topping: In a small bowl, combine the walnuts, the remaining 2 tablespoons of sugar, and the remaining ½ teaspoon of cinnamon. Remove the cake from the oven and, while it's still warm, sprinkle the walnut mixture over the top. Cool in the pan on a wire rack before packing.

perfect picnic beverages

GINGER TEA

Bring 4 cups of water to a boil. Add 4 tea bags and a 1-inch piece of fresh gingerroot. Steep for 5 minutes. Sweeten with sugar if desired. Chill completely and serve over ice.

HOMEMADE LEMON-LIMEADE

In a medium saucepan, combine 4 cups water and 1 cup sugar. Set over high heat and simmer for 1 minute, until the sugar melts. Remove from the heat and add 1 cup fresh lemon juice and $1/2$ cup fresh lime juice. Chill completely and serve over ice.

PASSION FRUIT PUNCH

In a blender, combine 2 cups orange juice, 1 cup diced mango, 1 cup pineapple chunks, and $1/2$ cup passion fruit nectar. Process until smooth. Serve over ice.

PINEAPPLE-APRICOT NECTAR

Combine 2 cups seltzer water, 2 cups pineapple juice, 2 cups cranberry juice, $1/4$ cup fresh lime juice, and one 11.5-ounce can apricot nectar. Serve over ice.

ROSEMARY-CHAMOMILE TEA

Bring 4 cups of water to a boil. Add 4 chamomile tea bags and 2 sprigs of fresh rosemary. Steep for 5 minutes. Sweeten with sugar if desired. Chill completely and serve over ice.

SUN TEA WITH MINT

In a glass container, combine 4 cups water, 4 tea bags, the rind from 1 whole lemon, and $1/4$ cup fresh mint leaves. Set the container in the sun for 6 to 8 hours. For a quicker version, bring the water to a boil first, add the tea bags, lemon rind, and mint, and steep for 5 minutes. Sweeten with sugar if desired. Chill completely and serve over ice.

WATERMELON CRUSH

In a blender, combine 2 cups cubed seeded watermelon and 2 tablespoons fresh lime juice. Process until smooth. Transfer to a thermos, then add 1 cup lemon-lime soda and 1 cup ice cubes.

picnic theme-party menus

SPRING'S ARRIVAL

Soft-Shell Crab Sandwiches with Almond Mayonnaise
(page 32)

Minty Cucumber Salad (page 20)

Zucchini Bread with Lemon (page 69)

SOCCER-MOM SOIREES

Smoky Chicken Fingers with Creamy
Honey-Mustard Dip (page 12)

Mango Salad with Tomatoes and
Red Onion (page 21)

Garden-Fresh Tortellini Salad (page 41)

Toffee-Chocolate Bars with Cashews (page 77)

SWIM-MEET SNACKS

Grilled Chicken and Swiss with Pesto on
Sourdough (page 37)

Pasta Spirals with Roasted Cherry Tomatoes
and Goat Cheese (page 44)

Blueberry Corn Muffins (page 88)

BEACH PARTY

Curried Crabmeat Salad (page 48)

Onion and Black Pepper Flatbread (page 72)

Tropical Fruit Salad with Coconut (page 83)

Chocolate-Dunked Coconut Macaroons (page 78)

POOLSIDE PARTY

Creamy Basil Pesto Dip (page 57)

Walnut-Cheddar Crisps (page 65)

Smoked Salmon Wrap with Chèvre,
Red Onion, and Lemon (page 27)

Couscous Salad with Peas and
Pearl Onions (page 45)

Pecan Squares (page 76)

JULY FOURTH BLOWOUT

Spicy Black Bean Dip (page 59)

Cumin-Dusted Pita Wedges (page 68)

Chicken Salad with Raspberries and Walnuts
(page 47)

Red Potato Salad with Bacon and
Fresh Herbs (page 14)

Hazelnut Half-Moon Cookies (page 81)

AUTUMN'S DEPARTURE

Coriander Peanut Sauce with Crudités (page 17)

Honey Ham Wrap with Gruyère, Endive, and
Coarse Mustard (page 29)

Apple-Cinnamon Coffee Cake (page 90)

mini picnics

ALMOST AMALFI

For a quick Italian antipasto basket, pack jars of roasted red peppers, artichoke hearts, marinated carrots and cauliflower, olives, and hot peppers. Add a loaf of crusty bread. Assemble the vegetables on a large plate when you're ready to eat.

AMERICAN STAPLES

For a traditional picnic, pack into a cooler fried chicken, potato salad, coleslaw, and cubed watermelon. Don't forget the red-checkered tablecloth!

ITALIAN COUNTRYSIDE

Pack into a basket or cooler a nice Italian cheese (Parmigiano Reggiano, Gorgonzola, Taleggio), a crusty loaf of bread, thinly sliced salami or Parma ham, and cubed honeydew melon.

PARIS IN THE PARK

Pack into a basket or cooler thinly sliced ham, Brie or Camembert, a baguette, and ripe pears.

setting the stage

The basket is packed and you've finally found the ideal, ant-free parcel of land you will call home for the next few hours. The "table"ware you select can help determine the perfect picnic menu.

ALL-AMERICAN PICNIC

WHAT TO BRING

A checkered cloth; red, white, and blue paper napkins; paper plates; plastic forks.

RECIPE SUGGESTIONS

Chilled Meat Loaf Sandwiches with Spicy Ketchup
　　(page 34)
Red Potato Salad with Bacon and Fresh Herbs
　　(page 14)
Oatmeal Raisin Cookies (page 80)

ELEGANT SOIREE

WHAT TO BRING

Cloth napkins and napkin rings, a blanket
and pillows, stemware, china plates, your finest
polished silver.

RECIPE SUGGESTIONS

Smoked Salmon with Caper Sour Cream and
   Black Bread (page 16),
Walnut-Cheddar Crisps (page 65)
Almond Biscotti (page 89)

ASIAN OUTING

WHAT TO BRING

Chopsticks, paper containers to hold the food
(transfer the food into these once you get there—not
before packing the cooler), fortune cookies.

RECIPE SUGGESTIONS

Thai Noodles with Vegetables and Peanuts
   (page 13)
Spicy Sesame Noodles (page 43),
Sesame-Glazed Shrimp Salad with Sugar Snap Peas
   (page 50)
Tropical Fruit Salad with Coconut (page 83)
Ginger Tea (page 92)

MEXICAN FIESTA

WHAT TO BRING

A red and green blanket, margaritas,
margarita glasses.

RECIPE SUGGESTIONS

White Bean and Ham Salad with Avocado and
   Lemon Vinaigrette (page 52)
Cheddar Corn Bread with Green Chilies (page 71)
Blueberry Corn Muffins (page 88)
Cumin-Dusted Pita Wedges (page 68) with the Spicy
   Black Bean Dip (page 59)

MIDDLE EASTERN EVENING

WHAT TO BRING

A colorful blanket, copper-colored serving utensils
(plastic is fine), candles.

RECIPE SUGGESTIONS

Coriander Peanut Sauce with Crudités
   (page 17)
Vegetarian Pita Pockets with Hummus, Marinated
   Eggplant, and Baby Greens (page 33)
Hazelnut Half-Moon Cookies (page 81)